JOURNEY INTO CIVILIZATION
THE MONGOLS

by Robert Nicholson

CHELSEA JUNIORS
A division of Chelsea House Publishers
New York • Philadelphia

Editorial consultant: Dr Christopher Cullen
School of Oriental and African Studies
University of London

This edition published 1994 by Chelsea House Publishers, a division of Main Line Book Co.
300 Park Avenue South, New York, N.Y. 10010 by arrangement with Two-Can Publishing Ltd.
This edition copyright © Two-Can Publishing Ltd., 1994

First published in Great Britain in 1992 by Two-Can Publishing Ltd., 346 Old Street, London EC1V 9NQ
Original edition © Two-Can Publishing Ltd 1992

1 3 5 7 9 8 6 4 2

ISBN 0-7910-2706-6
ISBN 0-7910-2730-9 (pbk.)

Contents

All words that appear in **bold** can be found in the glossary.

Russia

Aral
Sea

Caspian Sea

Iran

Hindu Kush

The Mongol World

The Mongols were fierce, warlike people who
originally came from the **steppes**
of central Asia. In the twelfth century, the
Mongols spread west into Muslim empires,
northwest into Russia, east into China and
eventually southeast into India, conquering the
local people as they went. At its largest, the
Mongol empire was bigger than any other
empire in history. The Mongols were the first
people to link Europe in the west with China
and the east, and they helped open vital trade
routes between east and west.

Pakistan

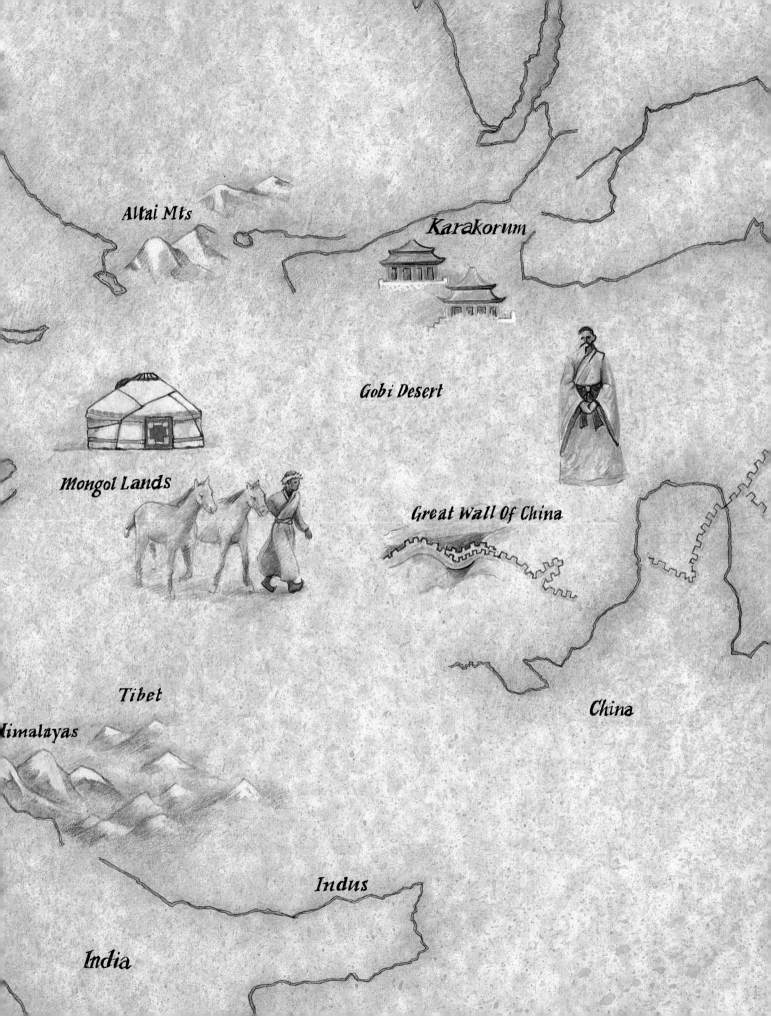

Altai Mts

Karakorum

Gobi Desert

Mongol Lands

Great Wall Of China

Tibet

China

Himalayas

Indus

India

The Steppes

The Mongols' homeland was a harsh and unforgiving land. In winter, the rolling grasslands, or steppes, were swept by icy Siberian winds. In summer, it was unrelentingly hot.

The Mongols were **nomads**. This means that they moved from one campsite to another to find better weather or conditions. There were few villages or towns. The Mongols had herds of goats, cows and horses but did not grow any crops.

In summer, they let their animals graze on the high flat plains, using the same grazing areas year after year. In winter, when it started to get cold, they moved down to the river valleys where it was warmer and sheltered from the viciously cold north winds.

▲ The Mongols were not **self-sufficient**. They traded with merchants and neighboring countries for grain, tea, fabrics and metals.

▶ Plenty of rain falls on the flat plains south of the Gobi Desert, making them ideal grazing land.

Horsemen and Warriors

Warfare and fighting were an important part of Mongol life. All men were taught to fight and use weapons. There were many different tribes on the steppes and they often clashed fiercely, fighting one another over grazing land or horses.

When all these tribes were united under the great Mongol leader **Genghis Khan**, they became a very strong army. They were harder and tougher than any of the enemies they met in Europe, China or Asia and could move more quickly on their strong little horses. They organized their army into a system of regiments, just like a modern army. Each man was part of a group of ten men. These groups were in turn joined into larger groups. All officers were given special gold tablets, called **paitzes**, which proved to everyone that they were officers, even to the lowest soldiers who could not read.

▲ The Mongols were superb horsemen. Their horses were their most important possessions. Most men had two or three horses so that they could keep riding when one tired. The horses were trained to follow each other. The Mongols usually rode mares so that their milk could be drunk in emergencies. The horses were short, but strong and stocky and had broad heads.

In their saddlebags, Mongols carried some food, a cooking pot, clothes, fishing line and tools for fixing and sharpening weapons. Their waterproof saddlebags could be blown up and used as a life jacket for crossing rivers.

Weapons

Bows were the main Mongol weapon. They were very powerful and accurate, and the Mongols were expert at using them even on horseback. The bows were beautifully crafted from sinew and horn, which made them more powerful than even the longbows used by medieval bowmen in England. They were carried with the string loose and only strung tight when they were in use.

Mongol warriors carried two quivers containing different sorts of arrows, some for piercing armor, some for shooting long distances, some with whistles for signaling and others for setting fire to enemy tents or towns.

Mongol horsemen also carried a sword, a javelin and sometimes an ax.

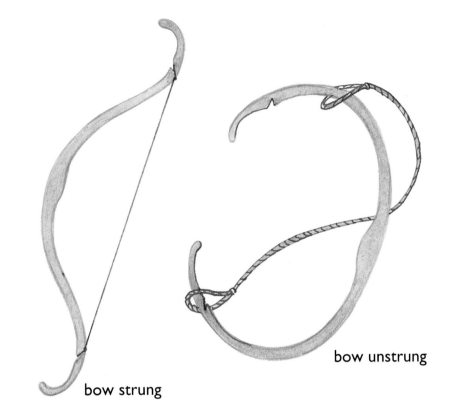

bow strung

bow unstrung

Genghis Khan

The Mongols were only one of the tribes of nomads on the steppes. Under their chief, Genghis Khan, they defeated their neighbors. They forced the other nomadic tribes to call themselves Mongols. Led by Genghis Khan and the **khans** after him, the Mongols established a huge empire.

The Mongols took advantage of the discoveries that had been made by the advanced countries that they conquered. Later Mongol armies made use of gunpowder and elaborate machinery for siege warfare.

▲ Trade was very important throughout the Mongol empire. Genghis Khan introduced a system of bank notes and coins.

Government

Genghis Khan found his huge empire hard to rule effectively. He set about developing a system of government to make things easier.

Mongol law was based on custom. There were no laws written down. In fact, the Mongols did not even have an alphabet or a system of writing of their own! The code of laws that Genghis introduced was called the **Yassa**. All the old customs were made into laws and strictly enforced. Lawbreakers were often harshly punished. Laws were introduced governing everything from taking slaves to stealing cattle.

▼ In order to write these laws down, the Mongols first had to learn to write. Genghis's sons were taught by one of their prisoners, using the alphabet of the Uighur tribe.

▲ When Genghis Khan conquered another tribe, they became part of his empire and were expected to obey Mongol law. However, Genghis was a fair ruler who allowed his subjects to carry on with their own life-styles and religions. In this painting, Genghis is speaking to some conquered people from the pulpit of a mosque.

The Yam

Because the empire was so huge it was important to be able to pass messages from one part to another. A postal system was started called the **Yam**. Along all the important routes there were staging posts where the royal messengers could get fresh horses, food and rest.

Religion

The Mongols had a sort of religion, but it was not written down, it did not have many rules and there was no public worship.

Tengri was the main god, the god of heaven. Below him was the earth goddess, **Itugan**, who controlled the fertility of herds and plants. Below her were other spirits, all controlling some aspect of nature and living things.

Priests were called **shamans.** They helped to reach the spirits through chanting, dreaming and ceremonies. They wore decorated white clothes and rode white horses so that everyone knew who they were.

The Mongols were very tolerant of other religions. Jews, Christians, Muslims and Buddhists were allowed to practice their own religion even when their lands had been conquered by the Mongols. In fact, some khans converted to the religion of the areas they had conquered.

The Sacred Elements

● Water was sacred because the springs and rivers were thought to represent powers that people had no control over.

● Fire was also sacred and was used to purify things.

● Daily prayers were said to the sun, the winds and the four points of the compass.

● The Mongols were buried with valuable possessions in secret graves, which were usually in the person's favorite place.

● A sheep's shoulder blade was thrown into the fire to make predictions. Vertical cracks were a good omen and horizontal ones were not.

Oboks

A Mongol tribe was divided into clans, called **oboks**, who made their own camps, and had their own leaders. The members of an obok hunted, fought and traveled together. Usually all the men in the obok were related, but wives came from another clan. Wives were often stolen from other clans, along with horses and cattle. Some men had several wives.

When a father died his possessions passed to the youngest son of his chief wife. He would also inherit his father's wives, which gave them protection and security after their husband's death.

Often smaller, weaker tribes would befriend a larger, stronger tribe so that they would save themselves from being attacked. A tribal leader was the absolute commander in wartime. In peacetime, he would advise and help settle disputes.

Nokers

A successful leader could persuade men to leave their own obok and join his. An oath of brotherhood kept a man in a new obok, and this was considered as strong as family ties. Men who had taken this oath were known as **nokers**. In this way, a man like Genghis Khan built up his huge following.

The Camp

Each family lived in a big felt tent called a **yurt**, or **ger**. The yurts were set up in a sheltered spot near a stream or river. When the obok moved campsites, large yurts were not dismantled. They were lifted up carefully onto huge frames with wheels. Then they were pulled along by oxen to the new site. The obok moved whenever its horses needed new grazing land or when the weather grew cold.

Large pieces of felt were stitched together and stretched over the frame. The felt was greased to make it watertight and windproof.

The frame of the yurt was made of wooden poles lashed together with rope.

Women's Work

The women were responsible for taking care of the herds of cows and goats. They also cooked all the food, made clothes and repaired the tents. Only the men were allowed to milk the horses because they were considered sacred.

The women were a very important part of the tribe. Their opinion was always asked on big issues, and they sometimes went to war with their husbands. There were even wives who became khans when their husbands died.

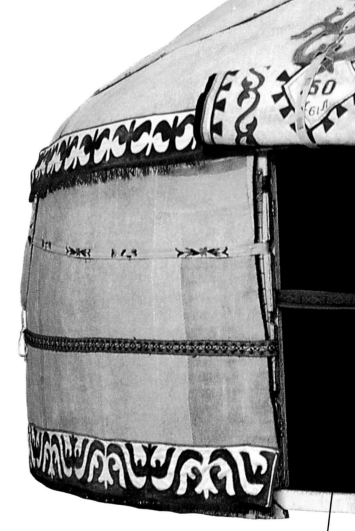

The entrance always faced south so that the cold north winds could not get in. A flap of felt was used as a door. It could be raised to air the yurt or lowered to keep in the warmth.

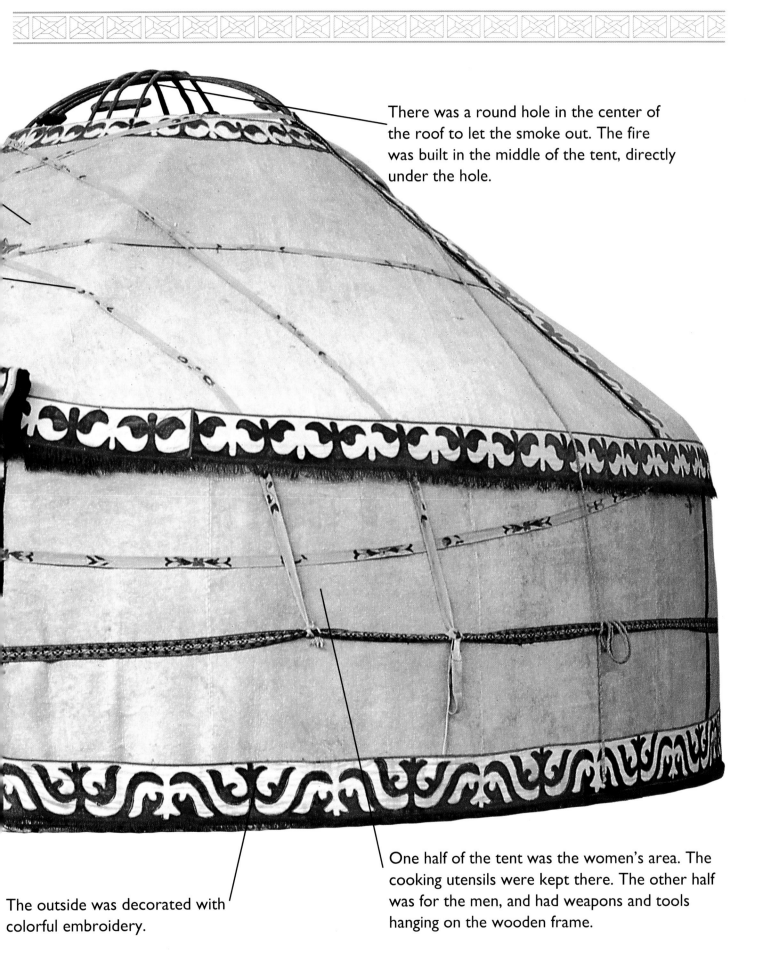

There was a round hole in the center of the roof to let the smoke out. The fire was built in the middle of the tent, directly under the hole.

The outside was decorated with colorful embroidery.

One half of the tent was the women's area. The cooking utensils were kept there. The other half was for the men, and had weapons and tools hanging on the wooden frame.

Food

The Mongols did not grow any of their own food. They bought rice, tea and other food from traders and merchants. When they could not trade, they had to rely on what was around them, so their food was mainly meat and milk.

Dogs, wolves, rats, mice, rabbits and occasionally horses were eaten, boiled or roasted. When the horsemen were on long raids, lasting several days with no time to stop and cook, raw meat was placed between the horse and saddle and eaten at the end of a day's riding when it had been tenderized. The Mongols said that grass was for horses and made men weak, so they did not eat many vegetables. The few they did eat grew wild, such as leeks, garlic and onions.

Food Facts

● **Kumiz** was a nutritious and highly alcoholic drink made from fermented mares' milk. Mongols often got drunk and were very proud of it.

● Running water was sacred, so the Mongols never washed themselves or their cooking utensils in it.

● **Charqui** was meat, dried by slicing it very thin and hanging it in the sun. It was eaten in the winter when food was more scarce. Meat was also made into dried sausages.

▶ This decorated Chinese bowl was made for the Mongols. Inside, it shows two merchants in Mongol costume. Most bowls would have been much plainer than this one.

19

Children

Children in Mongol tribes had lives that were completely different from the lives of children today. There were no schools and no spelling or math to do. However, the children did have a lot of other things to learn. Usually all children could ride horses by the age of five, so that they could travel when the obok moved camp.

Boys were taught by their fathers or uncles. They learned the skills of riding, how to make and mend saddles and bridles, how to milk mares and how to repair and make bows and arrows. All these were vital skills, just as important as reading and writing are today.

Girls were taught to take care of the camp by their mothers or older sisters. They learned how to cook, how to milk cows and goats, how to ride and how to make and repair their felt tents.

Mongol children of all ages loved to hear stories. These were told by grandmothers or old aunts. Most of these stories were tales of adventure on the steppes.

Mongols married at a very young age. Usually the boys were between 17 and 18 and the girls between 15 and 16. Weddings were arranged by parents and the celebrations sometimes lasted for three days.

Games

● Often children had no friends to play with. The steppes stretch a long way and campsites were often very far apart. Pets were very important. Dogs and small birds were the favorites.

● In winter, children played a game like ice hockey. An ankle bone from an ox was kicked around the ice, and points were scored depending on what position it landed in.

● In other games, pieces of bone were used as playing pieces.

Clothes

Both men and women wore a long sheepskin or fur-lined coat called a **del**. This buttoned down the front and was worn on top of an undershirt and leather pants. The front crossed over to keep out drafts. In winter, two coats were worn, one with the fur inwards and one with it facing outwards. A pouch containing chopsticks and flint for lighting fires was worn on the belt.

Mongol men wore hats made from silk or felt. Most hats were shaped like tight-fitting caps with a turned up brim all around, but there were lots of variations. Hats were generally trimmed with fur or decorated with a fan of feathers at the back. Most hats had a button, a spike or a tassel at the top. On their feet the men wore tall leather boots.

Mongol Fashion

⬤ Mongol soldiers scarred their faces and cheeks. This stopped the hair from growing so that they did not have to shave.

⬤ Young girls had long hair, married women cut their hair and shaved the sides of their heads and widows often shaved off all their hair.

⬤ Soldiers wore silk undershirts because an arrow could not pierce the tightly-knit woven silk. When a soldier was hit by an arrow, the silk could be gently pulled out, taking the arrow with it, without making the wound any worse.

⬤ A strong leather flap was attached to the back of a Mongol soldier's helmet. This protected his neck

▼ Silk was a useful fabric to the Mongols.

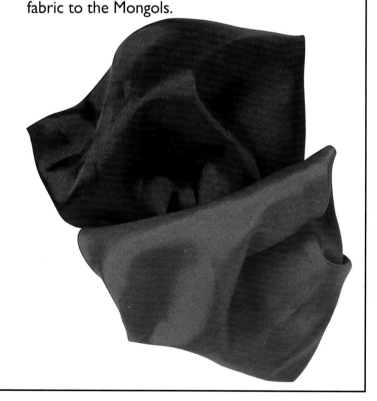

Make a Mongol Hat

Try making your own Mongol hat. Measure around your head. Cut two curved strips of lightweight cardboard just bigger than this measurement. Cut patterns in one of the strips, then stick the two strips together.

Now cut several shapes like the ones below. Curl over the tops and glue down.

Attach these pieces along the undecorated side of the long strips. Glue the ends of the hat together. Thread the wool through the loops and pull tight.

▼ Curl over the tops of the pieces.

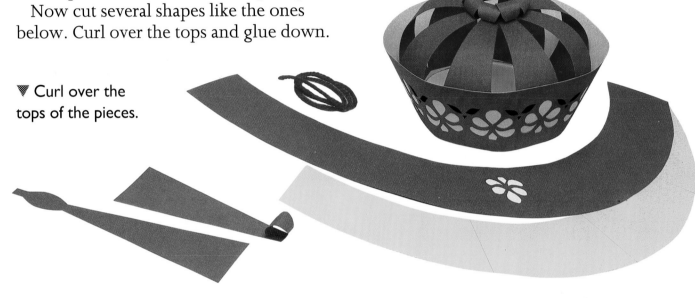

23

Crafts

Mongol life was hard and simple, but many of the everyday objects they made were beautifully crafted. Knives, belt buckles and bridles were decorated with silver. Shoes, saddles, boots and other clothes were often decorated with fine needlework. The Mongols were expert wood carvers and made beautiful chess sets, which were highly prized.

There is not very much left of the artefacts the Mongols made, although archaeologists are still discovering new things. For this reason, people often think that the Mongols were mere barbarians with no artistic skills. In fact, although they made few things themselves, the Mongols often encouraged and supported craftsmen in the lands they conquered. Kublai Khan, as emperor of China, set up a special government body to help craftsmen and excused them from paying some of their taxes. Craftsmen's children were not allowed to leave their father's trade. This ensured that crafts did not die out.

▲ This Persian tile shows two Mongol nobles.

▼ The paitzes that royal officials carried had simple designs on them so that even those who could not read were able to understand them. A commander of 10,000 men carried a gold paitze with a tiger's head carved on it.

▼ Genghis Khan's son Ogedei built a big palace in the capital Karakorum. It had gold fountains shaped like elephants, tigers and horses, with wine and kumiz pouring from their mouths.

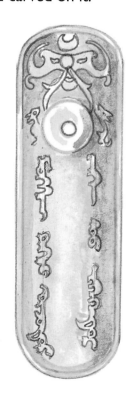

The Golden Knucklebone

The Mongols told many stories about the world around them. Although these stories are not true we can find out about the Mongols from them. This tale is about a Mongol boy and his wonderful horse.

Many years ago, on the steppes, there lived a boy called Altin who owned a golden knucklebone. Altin always won when he played knucklebones with the other children.

Altin's father bred horses to sell, and the family traveled around on the steppes, moving to places where the grass was better, or where there was a horse market.

One day, Altin's father drove his herd down to a pool to drink. He did not know that a magic Water Cat was lurking in the depths of the pool. The Water Cat put a spell on the horses, so that once their lips touched the water, they could not lift their heads.

"What is wrong with my horses?" shouted Altin's father.

With a great swish, the Water Cat rose from the water.

"I have trapped them! I will not let go until you give me Altin's golden knucklebone!"

"Yes, yes, just so long as you release my horses!" cried Altin's father. "I will leave the golden knucklebone in the ashes of our fire when we move camp tomorrow."

25

The Water Cat clapped his paws and disappeared. At once, the horses lifted their heads from the water again.

The next day, the family got up early to prepare to move camp. Altin did not notice his father carefully take the golden knucklebone and bury it in the ashes of the fire.

The family traveled for hours until they reached a place with fresh grass and a clear, cold stream. They began to set up camp at once. Then Altin realized that his golden knucklebone was missing. He asked everyone if they had seen it, but no one seemed to know where it was. Finally, Altin's mother told him that she had seen his father burying the golden knucklebone in the ashes of the fire at the old camp.

"I must go back and fetch it," replied Altin.

Altin looked around for a horse to ride. He picked up a bridle and shook it. A shaky little colt came staggering up to him.

"You're far too small, I can't ride you," said Altin, and he shook the bridle again. But no other horse came, so he shrugged his shoulders and put a saddle and bridle on the shaky little colt. No sooner had the saddle touched his back, than the colt turned into a magnificent strong horse. Altin leaped on to

the horse's back and they galloped off, faster than the wind, to the old camp. There, the Water Cat was sitting by the fire tossing the golden knucklebone from paw to paw.

"Give me back my golden knucklebone!" said Altin.

"Come and get it!" hissed the Water Cat.

Before the Water Cat had a chance to run off, the horse snatched the golden knucklebone in his teeth and galloped away. The Water Cat clapped his paws and another horse appeared. He leapt on its back and galloped after Altin.

Eventually Altin's horse could go no further. He gave Altin the golden knucklebone and told him to climb into a tree. Then the horse turned himself into a red fox and hid behind some bushes. When the Water Cat arrived and saw Altin, he clapped his paws and his horse turned into an ax. He began to chop the tree down. He had nearly chopped through the trunk, when the fox (who was really the horse) came out from behind the bushes.

"I'm very good at chopping," said the fox (who was really the horse). Can I help?"

So the Water Cat gave the fox his ax and lay down to sleep. While he slept, the fox blew on the tree until it was mended. Then he threw the ax away and hid in the bushes.

When the Water Cat woke up and saw the tree he was furious. Spitting with rage, he clapped his hands, and a new ax appeared. Then he began to chop the tree again. The fox (who was really the horse) changed his coat to black and came out from behind the bushes.

"Aren't you tired?" he said. "Let me help, I'm really good at chopping."

"Not you again," replied the Water Cat.

"No, no," said the black fox. "You must have met my brother. He's deceitful. But I won't let you down." So the Water Cat went to sleep and the fox mended the tree and then threw the ax away and hid in the bushes.

When the Water Cat woke up he was furious. He clapped his hands for a new ax, and chopped at the tree until it was nearly severed. Behind the bush, the fox changed his coat from black to white.

"Let me help," offered the white fox, coming out from behind the bushes.

"You're not going to trick me this time!" said the Water Cat, taking a swing at the tree.

From his perch, Altin could see that the tree was about to break. He sent a bird to his father's camp with a message for his two dogs.

Just as the Water Cat was about to take the last swing at the tree, he spotted a cloud of dust coming towards the tree very quickly.

"What can that be?" wondered the Water Cat, but in an instant the two dogs were upon him. They chased him around the tree, getting closer and closer until they finally chased him into the river.

Altin climbed down from the tree with the golden knucklebone safe in his hand, and thanked the horse and the two dogs. Then the horse breathed on the tree to mend its trunk again, and they all set off back to the camp.

When they arrived, Altin's mother and father had just finished setting up camp.

"What have you been up to?" they asked.

"Oh, nothing much," Altin replied.

How We Know

Have you ever wondered how we know so much about the Mongols, even though they lived so long ago?

Evidence from the Ground

The Mongols built few buildings, and left little else for us to remember them by. They were buried in secret graves, and not many works of their art survive. Even the only sizeable Mongol town, the old capital, Karakorum, has largely been destroyed.

Today in **Mongolia** archaeologists are still working on important sites, so more from the Mongol's world may yet to be discovered.

▲ This page is from a Chinese manuscript about Genghis Khan.

Evidence in Writing

There is only one surviving piece of Mongol literature from the period. This is the *Secret History of the Mongols*, which Genghis Khan instructed his sons to write. It is a useful source of information, although it is probably not very accurate.

Evidence from Enemies

European, Chinese and Persian writings are a valuable source of information about the Mongols. However, this information is often inaccurate because these people were at one time or another bitter enemies of the Mongols, and so what they wrote usually shows the Mongols in a very bad light.

▲ An Italian traveler named Marco Polo spent many years at the court of Kublai Khan. He wrote an account of his travels called *A Description of the World*, which paints a very clear picture of Mongol life. This painting shows Marco Polo leaving Venice.

Glossary

charqui
Dried meat eaten in winter.

del
The long coat worn by Mongol men and women.

Genghis Khan (1162-1227)
Mongol who first united the tribes and established the Mongol empire.

ger
A Mongol tent.

Itugan
Mongol goddess of fertility.

khan
The name used by all Mongol rulers.

kumiz
An alcoholic drink made from fermented mare's milk.

Mongolia
The country between Russia and China which includes much of the original Mongol lands.

noker
A member of a Mongol tribe who has taken an oath of brotherhood to that tribe.

nomad
A member of a wandering tribe.

obok
A small family group or clan who traveled together.

paitze
A golden tablet showing authority.

self-sufficient
To have one's own resources, such as food, cloth, tools and livestock.

shaman
A priest who helped send messages to the spirits.

steppes
The rugged grassy plains area in Asia.

Tengri
The main Mongol god.

Yam
The Mongol postal system.

Yassa
Mongol laws made official by Genghis Khan.

yurt
A Mongol tent.

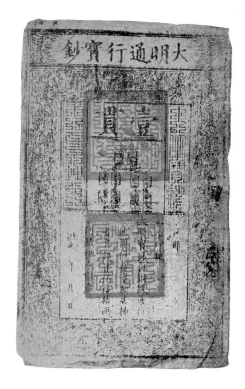

Index